The Holocaust

INVESTIGATIONS

Neil DeMarco

Hodder & Stoughton

A MEMBER OF THE HODDER HEADLINE GROUP

Acknowledgements

The front cover shows *Gassing* (detail) by David Olere, gift of the Olere family, Museum of Jewish Heritage, New York and a photo of Anne Frank, reproduced courtesy of AKG Photo London. David Olere was deported from Drancy to Auschwitz, March 2, 1943, no. 106144.

The publishers would like to thank the following individuals, institutions and companies for permission to reproduce copyright illustrations in this book:

AKG Photo London pages 4, 9 and 27; Associated Press AP page 5; Bundesarchiv, Koblenz page 6; Archives of the Wiener Library pages 12, 15, 19 and 21 (l) and 25 (l); Yad Vashem Photographic Library Jerusalem pages 13, 23 and 25 (r); Trial of Adolph Eichmann, courtesy of Rubin Mass Ltd., Jerusalem page 21 (r); Hulton Getty Picture Collection page 29.

The publishers would also like to thank the following for permission to reproduce material in this book:

BBC/Richard Dimbleby for the extract from the broadcast by Richard Dimbleby from Belsen on 19 April 1945; *The Holocaust* by Martin Gilbert, HarperCollins Publishers Ltd, 1987; Her Majesty's Stationery Office for the extract from *The Faber Book of Reportage* 1987, Ed. J Carey; Judith Jaegermann for an extract from *My Childhood in the Holocaust*; *This Way for the Gas, Ladies and Gentlemen* by Tadeusz Borowski selected and translated by Barbara Vedder (Originally published in Wybor Opowiadan, Pantswowy Instytyt Wydawniczy, Poland, 1959, Penguin Books 1976) copyright © Maria Borowski, 1959. This translation copyright © Penguin Books Ltd, 1967, reproduced by permission of Penguin Books Ltd; Penguin Putnam Inc. for the extract from *If this is a Man (Survival in Auschwitz)* by Primo Levi, Pocket Books, 1993; The Random House Group Ltd for the extract from Mein Kampf by Adolf Hitler, Pimloco; 'Never Forget' by L Morrow from *Time Magazine*, 26 April 1993.

Every effort has been made to trace and acknowledge ownership of copyright. The publishers will be glad to make suitable arrangements with any copyright holders whom it has not been possible to contact.

The author and publisher would like to thank the Education Departments of the Board of Deputies of British Jews and the London Jewish Cultural Centre for their advice.

Orders: please contact Bookpoint Ltd, 130 Milton Park, Abingdon, Oxon OX14 4SB. Telephone: (44) 01235 827720, Fax: (44) 01235 400454. Lines are open from 9.00 – 6.00, Monday to Saturday, with a 24 hour message answering service. Email address: orders@bookpoint.co.uk

British Library Cataloguing in Publication Data
A catalogue record for this title is available from The British Library

ISBN 0 340 79979 X

First published 2001
Impression number   10 9 8 7 6 5 4 3 2 1
Year   2005 2004 2003 2002 2001

Copyright © 2001 Neil DeMarco

Typeset by Liz Rowe.
Printed in Italy for Hodder & Stoughton Educational, a division of Hodder Headline Plc, 338 Euston Road, London NW1 3BH.

Contents

1 WHY DID THE NAZIS MURDER ANNE FRANK? (Part 1)

CHECK OUT THE LINK
Why did Hitler hate the Jews? (Chapter 3)
Why was there so little opposition to the Holocaust? (Chapter 10)

At 11 a.m. on August 4, 1944, five or six members of the Nazi secret police, the Gestapo, and local Dutch Nazis arrived at the offices of 263 Prinsengracht. It was a warm, busy day and nobody in the building noticed the arrival of the motor car. The men opened the front door and went up the stairs. A man in civilian clothes opened the office door and pointed a pistol at the two office workers.

One of the Dutch Nazis said, 'We know everything. You are hiding Jews. Take us to them.'

The workers knew it was over and there was no escape. One of them, Victor Kugler, led the men upstairs and pointed to the bookcase at the end of the hall. The police moved the bookcase aside to reveal the secret door behind. The Gestapo officer motioned with his pistol for Kugler to go first. He made his way upstairs to the living room where the startled Jews were sitting.

'The Gestapo are here,' he said.

The Franks – Otto and Edith, and their two young daughters, Anne and Margot – stood with their hands up as the officer pointed his pistol at them. Margot was crying quietly. The Franks' long, ten-year struggle to escape the Nazis had finally ended. Within seven months all but Otto Frank would be dead.

NEW WORDS

ANNEXE: a building added onto another building, usually at the side or the back.
HOLOCAUST: the mass murder of Jews and other groups hated by the Nazis.
PERSECUTION: a campaign of attacks, often against groups who cannot defend themselves.
TYPHUS: a disease spread by fleas and body lice which leads to severe pain, fever and eventually the failure of vital organs such as the heart and kidneys.

Illustration of the Annexe. ▼

SOURCE A

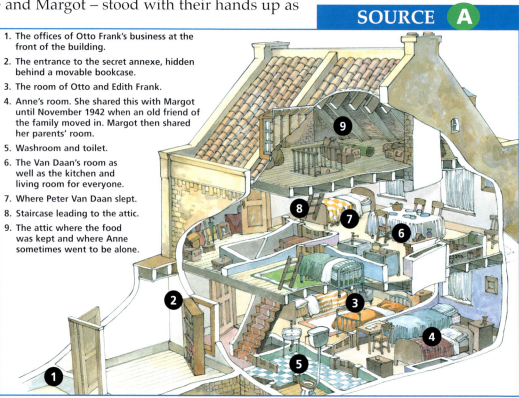

1. The offices of Otto Frank's business at the front of the building.
2. The entrance to the secret annexe, hidden behind a movable bookcase.
3. The room of Otto and Edith Frank.
4. Anne's room. She shared this with Margot until November 1942 when an old friend of the family moved in. Margot then shared her parents' room.
5. Washroom and toilet.
6. The Van Daan's room as well as the kitchen and living room for everyone.
7. Where Peter Van Daan slept.
8. Staircase leading to the attic.
9. The attic where the food was kept and where Anne sometimes went to be alone.

ESCAPE FROM NAZI GERMANY

In 1934 Otto and Edith Frank left Germany with their two daughters, Anne and Margot, to escape the Nazis. At this time the Nazis encouraged German Jews to emigrate – though they had to hand over property, businesses and possessions to the government before they left. The Franks chose Amsterdam in Holland. Six years later, in 1940, the Germans invaded Holland and the Franks were once again in danger.

Anne Frank was 11 years old, and her sister 14, when the Germans invaded Holland. Otto Frank began to make preparations for his family to go into hiding. He secretly converted the **annexe** of his business into a concealed hiding place. The annexe had two upper floors and an attic. None of this could be seen from outside because it was at the back of the business. The entrance inside to the annexe was hidden behind a moveable bookcase.

PERSECUTION

Gradually, the Nazi **persecution** of the Jews in Holland was stepped up. In September 1941 Anne was stopped from going to the same school as her non-Jewish friends. From May 1942 all Jews in Holland had to wear a yellow Star of David sewn onto their clothing so that people would know they were Jews. Jews couldn't ride on trams, go to the cinema or even ride a bicycle. They were allowed to shop for just two hours every day. Some shop owners refused to serve them. In July of that year Margot was told she would be sent to a 'work camp' in Germany and it was then that Otto decided they would have to go into hiding in their secret annexe on July 9, 1942. His business partner and his wife and 16-year-old son, Peter, joined them, making seven. Eventually, one more would join them in the cramped accommodation.

LIFE IN THE ANNEXE

None of those living in the annexe could leave it again as long as the Germans were in Holland. Everything they needed – food and supplies – was smuggled to them secretly by the four people who knew where they were. These were all employees in Otto's business – two Dutch men and two Dutch women, Miep and Bep. These four risked their lives by helping the people in the annexe.

None of the other workers in Otto Frank's business knew that the Franks were hiding in the annexe so the hidden family had to be especially quiet during the day. They could not use the lavatory or turn on taps during office hours in case someone heard the noise. There were big rewards from the Germans for Dutch people who informed on or betrayed Jews who were in hiding to the police.

ARREST

Just a month before the Franks went into the annexe, Anne had been given a diary as a thirteenth birthday present. She called her diary 'Kitty' and all her entries in the diary talk to Kitty as though she were writing to a real friend. She became fond of the 16-year-old boy, Peter, who had the room above her.

Anne excitedly told her diary of their first real kiss on April 28, 1944 (see **Source C**). Her last entry is for August 1, 1944. Three days later, the German and Dutch police arrived at the house. They knew the Franks were hidden there. They had been tipped off but nobody knows who told the police.

All eight people were taken to a transit camp and a month later, in September 1944, they were taken by train to Auschwitz. On arrival, children who looked under the age of 15 were gassed. Anne, who was 15 and three months, was selected for work, along with her sister and mother. She was separated from her father and Peter and never saw them again. Peter did not survive the war.

Think about it …

- Design a storyboard for a film about Anne Frank.
- Decide what events to portray.
- Write a brief description of each scene.
- Provide a simple sketch to show what will be seen in each scene.

WHY DID THE NAZIS MURDER ANNE FRANK? (Part 2)

DEATH

After a month Anne and Margot were moved to another camp, Bergen-Belsen. Their mother, Edith, was kept behind. She died in Auschwitz in January, 1945, just three weeks before the Russian army freed the prisoners. Among those who survived was Otto but not Peter. Margot died of **typhus** in March, 1945. Anne, convinced her parents were both dead, and lost without her sister, gave in to the same disease and died a few days later. The following month British soldiers reached the camp. Anne had been just a few weeks from survival.

THE DIARY

Anne's diary had been rescued by Miep from the rooms wrecked by the police. She gave it to Otto when he finally made his way back to Amsterdam in June 1945. He decided he would have it published but it wasn't easy to find a publisher so soon after the war. Eventually, 1,500 copies were printed in 1947. Today, it has been published in 55 languages and has sold over 20 million copies. The annexe to Anne's house is now a museum. The 14-year-old girl who told her diary that she wanted to go on living after her death has achieved that and much more. Anne was just one of the 1 and a half million Jewish children who perished in the **Holocaust**.

'IT COULDN'T HAPPEN HERE …'

The story of Anne Frank and her family is a terrible one. But the fact that it happened more than 50 years ago perhaps makes it a little less shocking, a little less disturbing. After all, it was a long time ago and these things don't happen today, at the start of a new century, do they? Even if similar events do happen, we tell ourselves, they happen in poor, faraway countries like Rwanda and not in modern, advanced places like Europe.

SOURCE B

▲ *Anne Frank.*

However, events in Bosnia and in Kosovo in the 1990s show us that terrible crimes against defenceless people can just as easily happen in modern Europe as anywhere else.

SOURCE C

At half-past eight I stood up and went to the window where we always say goodbye … He came towards me, I flung my arms round his neck and gave him a kiss on his left cheek, and was about to kiss the other cheek, when my lips met his and we pressed them together. In a while we were clasped in each other's arms, again and again, never to leave off.

▲ *From* The Diary of Anne Frank, *entry dated 28 April 1944.*

HOW DO THESE THINGS HAPPEN?

What these terrible events have in common is hatred – the hatred of the people carrying out the crimes against their victims. But the fact that the Nazis hated the Jews, or Serbs hated the Muslims of Bosnia or Kosovo doesn't explain enough. Other factors must also be involved if the persecutors are to succeed in their aims:

■ The people carrying out the crimes must not only hate but they must believe that what they are doing is *right*. Their reasons might be to do with religion or race or they might feel that their victims threaten their way of life or beliefs.

■ The victims must be defenceless and isolated, unable to get help from *others*.

■ Perhaps most importantly of all, the people who could do something to stop disaster from happening don't do anything. These people might be those who live in the same community, or they might be the governments of other countries.

HOW DO THESE THINGS START?

Prejudice – the dislike of something or someone without a good reason – exists everywhere in society and in many different forms. There is prejudice against people because they are a different colour or come from a different country, because they are a different sex or because they have a disability or a different religion. Civilised societies create laws to prevent people like these from becoming victims of such prejudice. Your school has these rules too.

When these rules are ignored and not enforced, then the weaker or defenceless members of the community are at risk. At first, maybe the attacks are not too serious – perhaps some name-calling. But if this isn't stopped by those who *can* do something about it, it gets more serious. Name-calling can be followed by bullying and soon a person's life becomes a misery.

In Germany, as we shall see, the Nazis began their persecution of the Jews very gradually. They urged Germans not to buy from Jewish shops for just *one* day or not to use a Jewish dentist or doctor. Most Germans didn't protest about these measures. Ordinary Germans, who could have defended the Jews, chose not to. The next stage of the Nazi campaign was more serious. The process which eventually led to the gas chambers had started.

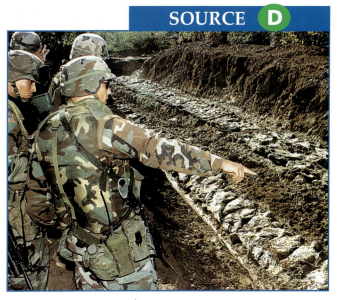

▲ *A massacre discovered in Bosnia in 1998.*

Q **1.** Show how the Nazis *gradually* stepped up their persecution of the Jews in Holland.

2. Why do you think they did it this way rather than send them to concentration camps straight away?

3. Can you think of a reason why Otto Frank found it so difficult to find a publisher so soon after the war?

4. How do entries like the one in **Source C** help to explain the popularity of Anne's diary?

5. Describe a situation today in which a schoolchild gradually becomes a victim of other people's prejudice. This can be real or made up. Show how the three points listed above left apply to this situation.

2 THE HISTORY WEB: HOW AND WHY DID THE HOLOCAUST HAPPEN?

This book sets out to answer one big question: 'How and why did the Holocaust happen?' The answer to a question like this is made up of several other questions which connect to this big question, and some of these questions are also linked to each other. In a way, the whole investigation is a bit like a giant spider's web, like the one you can see on the next page.

A question as complex as this one needs a close investigation of the events before and after. It's important to understand that the **anti-Semitism** which led to the Holocaust had existed in Europe for at least 1,000 years. Hitler and his National Socialist Party (or Nazi Party for short) made this hatred of Jews a vital part of their political ideas. The fact that the Nazi Party was the most popular party in Germany in the early 1930s shows that many other Germans shared Hitler's anti-Semitism.

One of the most puzzling issues we will investigate is why the Nazis were able to get away with it. Why didn't the German people try to help the Jews? Did anybody try to help them? Did the Jews resist? Why did the Nazis get the support of people in the countries they had just conquered?

SOURCE A

▲ A policeman closes the car door for a couple of German officers on their way to the German Headquarters. If the uniform of the policeman looks familiar, it's not really surprising. This is a British policeman in Guernsey, one of the Channel Islands occupied by the Germans in 1940. About 60,000 British citizens lived under German occupation during the war. The British authorities in the Channel Islands behaved in much the same way as the authorities did in other parts of Europe controlled by the Germans. They obeyed German laws and co-operated in identifying to the Germans those Jews who lived in the islands. Some of these perished in the death camps. British women had love affairs with German soldiers and friendships were made. Most Britons worked for the Germans in some way, but then they did pay good wages. Remember this the next time you say to yourself, 'It couldn't happen here.'

SOURCE **B**

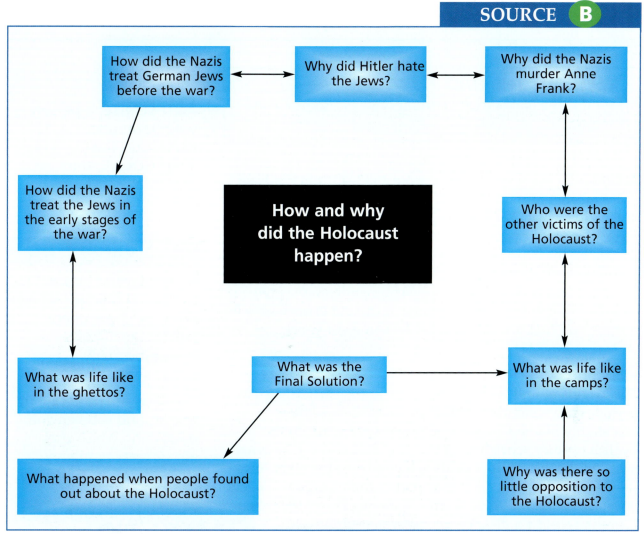

▲ *How and why did the Holocaust happen web.*

Answering questions like these will lead us towards a better understanding of just how this terrible crime could be committed in the middle of the twentieth century.

However, the study of history is not just about the past. It's about the future too. There are lessons to be learned from the past. The circumstances which led to the Holocaust in the 1940s can easily reoccur – though the Jews may not be the victims again. Muslims in countries like Bosnia and Serbia will tell you that they too have been the victims of a terrible campaign of mass-murder and that this was during the *1990s*. One of the purposes of this book is to make you aware of just how these events came about so that future generations can ensure that they are not repeated.

Look at **Source B**. This is a history web which shows all the questions we will answer and how these questions fit together to make an overall picture. The big investigation is 'How and why did the Holocaust happen?' To explore this question we need to fit together several smaller investigations, such as 'Why did Hitler hate the Jews?' and 'Why was there so little opposition to the Holocaust?'.

Q

Think about it...
■ Look at the history web in **Source B**. Choose three of the smaller investigations which you think are important in explaining why the Holocaust happened and then explain what you think you might learn from each of these three investigations.

3 WHY DID HITLER HATE THE JEWS?

CHECK OUT THE LINK
How did the Nazis treat German Jews before the war? (Chapter 4)

Adolf Hitler, ruler of Germany from 1933–45, and his Nazi Party murdered more than half of Europe's 11 million Jews in the Holocaust. The vast majority of these murders took place in just four years from 1941 to 1945. Hitler was able to do this because his feelings of hatred towards the Jews (known as anti-Semitism) were shared by many other Germans and peoples in Europe. Anti-Semitism was not invented by Hitler or the Germans. It existed everywhere in Europe and had been around for hundreds of years.

MEDIEVAL ANTI-SEMITISM

The origins of anti-Semitism go back to the early Christian period. Early Christians hated the Jews because they mistakenly blamed them for killing Jesus Christ. In the twelfth century, Christian hatred was made worse by what is called the 'blood libel'. This is the untrue story that Jews sacrificed Christian children as part of their religious beliefs. Jews across all of Europe were sometimes murdered when Christian children disappeared or were found dead.

There are further examples of anti-Semitism in the Middle Ages. Jews were sometimes made to wear a yellow badge and were forced to live in separate parts of towns and cities called ghettos. Eventually, the rulers of England, France, Germany, Portugal and Spain ordered all the Jews to leave their countries. Many moved to Poland and Russia but persecution here led millions to move to the USA at the end of the nineteenth century.

MODERN ANTI-SEMITISM

By the early years of the twentieth century, anti-Semitism had become a race issue as well as a religious one. **Anti-Semites** now argued that Jews came from a lower race. This was a serious matter for Jews. While in medieval times, Jews who converted to Christianity and gave up Judaism were welcomed by Christians such as Luther (see **Source A**), to modern anti-Semites, converting to Christianity made no difference. Hitler shared this view and the Nazis treated Christian Jews with the same hatred as other Jews.

NEW WORDS
ANTI-SEMITE: a person who hates and persecutes Jews.
SYNAGOGUE: the Jewish place of worship.

SOURCE A

Martin Luther was a German monk. His views on Jews, shown here, written in 1543, were shared by many Christians:

The Jews are nothing but thieves and robbers and everything which they eat or wear has been stolen from us. Thus they live from day to day, together with wife and child, by theft and robbery. We let them get rich on our sweat and blood, while we remain poor and they suck the marrow from our bones. What shall we Christians do with this rejected and condemned people, the Jews?

First, set fire to their **synagogues** or schools and bury and cover with dirt whatever will not burn. Second, I advise that their houses also be destroyed.

▲ *From* Luther's Works, *Volume 47:* The Christian in Society IV.

SOURCE B

Like leeches, the Jews slowly suck the blood from the pores of the people … The Jew is a parasite, a sponger who, like an evil virus, spreads over wider and wider areas … The effect is also like that of a vampire … wherever he lives the people who welcome him are bound to be bled to death sooner or later.

▲ *From* **Mein Kampf** *('My Struggle') by Adolf Hitler, written in 1924.*

HITLER'S ANTI-SEMITISM

In the 1920s and 1930s Hitler blamed the Jews for Germany's defeat in the First World War and the humiliating Treaty of Versailles which followed it. Hitler had begun to hate the Jews during his years in Vienna before the First World War. He noticed how some Jews dressed differently, spoke their own language and had their own religion. To Hitler, they were just *different* and couldn't be 'proper' Germans. The Germans, according to Hitler, were a pure northern European race called Aryans. For Hitler, Germany could only become a great nation again if it remained racially pure. To do this, all traces of the Jews must be removed from German life. Hitler had similar views about Slav peoples (e.g. Russians and Poles) and blacks (see Chapter 8).

SOURCE C

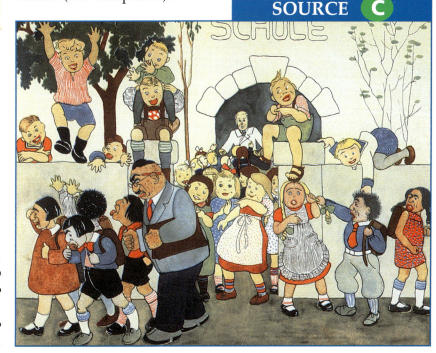

A cartoon from a Nazi ➤ *textbook for schoolchildren. It shows Jews being forced to leave the school they share with German Aryan children. The Jews are shown on the bottom left of the picture.*

Q

1. Why did some Christians hate the Jews?

2. What examples of anti-Semitism can you find in **Source A**?

3. In what ways are the attitudes towards the Jews in **Sources A** and **B** similar?

4. Look at **Source C**. How has the artist drawn the Jews compared with the Aryan children?

5. Why do you think Hitler's ideas about the Jews were so easily accepted by so many Germans? Think about:

■ The views of Christians about Jesus and the 'blood libel'.

■ How many Germans felt after their defeat in the First World War.

■ Hitler's promise to make Germany a great nation again.

Check out the link:
Look at Chapter 4. How did Hitler's views affect how Jews were treated once he came to power?

4 HOW DID THE NAZIS TREAT GERMAN JEWS BEFORE THE WAR?

CHECK OUT THE LINK
Why did Hitler hate the Jews? (Chapter 3)

NEW WORDS

BOYCOTT: to refuse to buy from, or use the services of, a particular group – in this case Germany's Jews.
CONCENTRATION CAMP: a prison where there was ill-treatment and beatings but not murder on the scale of the later death camps.
REPRISAL: an act of revenge.

Historians are not sure exactly what Hitler's *long-term* plans for the Jews were. It seems likely that Hitler didn't know either. But he didn't wait long before making a start on his anti-Semitic policies once he became Chancellor of Germany in 1933. These policies were mild compared to what the Nazis were to do later. Perhaps Hitler was uncertain how the policies would affect the German economy, and he may have been worried about the opinion of foreign governments if his measures were too violent. To begin with, then, Hitler moved cautiously.

BOYCOTT
On April 1, 1933, the Nazis called on Germans to **boycott** Jewish businesses and professionals, such as dentists and doctors. However, the boycott only lasted one day. Jews were also banned from working for the government or as doctors, dentists and lawyers.

Some Jews – with the Nazi government's approval – decided to leave Germany. During 1933 and 1934 60,000 out of Germany's 500,000 Jews left Germany for good – the Franks were among them. It wasn't easy, however, to find countries willing to let them in. Nonetheless, by the time Hitler stopped Jews from leaving Germany in 1941, 75 per cent had left the country.

THE NUREMBERG LAWS
Many fanatical Nazis were unhappy with the slow progress of the measures against the Jews. They wanted harsher policies. In 1935 Hitler decided to give them what they wanted. The Nuremberg Laws:

- Banned marriages and sexual relations between Jews and non-Jews.
- Stopped Jews from being German citizens.
- Stopped Jews from using public facilities such as swimming pools and restaurants.

Most Germans didn't appear to be very concerned about what was happening to the Jews. In fact, many Germans seemed to welcome these laws. Most Jews simply hoped that things wouldn't get any worse and 'kept their heads down'. But they did get worse.

NIGHT OF BROKEN GLASS
On November 7, 1938, a 17-year-old Polish Jew shot dead a German diplomat in Paris in protest against the German government's anti-Semitism. The Nazi leaders quickly organised a wave of anti-Jewish **reprisals** in which over 8,000 Jewish businesses and 200 synagogues were destroyed. Over 30,000 Jewish men were arrested and sent to **concentration camps**. Most of these were released within a couple of months but not before about 1,000 had been murdered.

EUTHANASIA
One Nazi policy which did lead to protests inside Germany was euthanasia – the mass killing of physically and mentally handicapped Germans. The Nazis had already begun a policy of sterilising these people so that they couldn't have children, but euthanasia went a step further. Between the autumn of 1939 and August 1941 70,000

men, women and children had been killed for these reasons. Hitler was determined to make the German people a 'master race' (*Herrenvolk*). This master race would have blue eyes and blonde hair, and no physical or mental weaknesses. There would, therefore, be no place for the handicapped. Many of the victims were gassed with carbon monoxide. The government tried to keep the programme secret but details soon leaked out. A protest by a leading German Catholic bishop in August 1941 forced Hitler temporarily to stop the policy. It was soon restarted but in greater secrecy.

SOURCE B

▲ *Illustration of the Nazi campaign against the Jews, 1933–39.*

SOURCE A

The doctor in charge said 'We do not carry out the action [euthanasia] with poison, injections, or other measures which can be recognised … for then the foreign press … would have new opportunities for propaganda against us … No, our method is much simpler.'

With these words he pulled a child out of its cot … He displayed the whimpering skeleton-like little person like a hare which had just been caught. 'Naturally, we don't stop their food straight away. That would cause too much fuss. We gradually reduce their portions. Nature then takes care of the rest … This one won't last more than two or three days.'

▲ *A description of a visit in 1940 by some leading Nazis to a children's asylum where euthanasia was carried out.*

Q

1. Using **Source B** as a guide, explain how the Nazi campaign against the Jews developed between 1933 and 1938.

2. Some Jews actually began to return to Germany in 1936 and 1937. Look at **Source B**. Can you suggest why?

3. Imagine you are a Jewish child in Germany in 1938. Write a letter to a friend explaining how Hitler has affected your life and that of your family:

■ Mention Nazi ideas about the Jews.

■ Show how these ideas have affected Jews.

■ Explain why Hitler's policies have sometimes changed.

■ Sum up by saying what life is like in 1938 and what your fears (or hopes) are for the future.

5 HOW DID THE NAZIS TREAT THE JEWS IN THE EARLY STAGES OF THE WAR?

CHECK OUT THE LINK
What was life like in the *ghettos*? (Chapter 6)

SOURCE A

Without weeping or crying these people stood together in family groups, embracing each other and saying goodbye … An old woman with snow-white hair held a one-year-old child in her arms singing to it and tickling it. The child squeaked with delight. The married couple looked on with tears in their eyes. The father held the ten-year-old boy by the hand speaking softly to him. The boy was struggling to hold back his tears. The father pointed a finger to the sky and stroked his head and seemed to be explaining something to him … I can still remember how a girl, slender and dark, pointed at herself as she went past me saying 'twenty-three'.

The people, completely naked, climbed down steps which had been cut into the clay wall of the ditch, stumbled over the heads of those lying there and stopped at the spot indicated by the **SS** man. They lay down on top of the dead or wounded; some stroked those still living and spoke quietly to them. Then I heard a series of rifle shots. I looked into the ditch and saw the bodies contorting or, the heads already motionless, sinking on the corpses beneath. Blood flowed from the nape of their necks.

I am making the above statement in Wiesbaden, Germany on 10 November 1945. I swear to God that it is the whole truth.

▲ *A German engineer's eye witness account of a massacre of Jews in the Ukraine, in October 1942.*

NEW WORDS

GHETTO: a small, sealed-off section of a town or city in which Jews were forced to live.
SS (SCHUTZSTAFFEL): Defence squad. This was a section of the Nazi Party reserved for only the most loyal and fanatical supporters of Hitler.

A group of Jewish men, women and children stands at the edge of a pit, waiting to be shot. One of the children takes a last look at the horror behind her. ▼

SOURCE B

A group of Jewish women and children, stripped of their clothes, wait their turn for execution, August 1942. ➤

SOURCE C

THE MADAGASCAR PLAN

Nazi policy towards the Jews in the early stages of the war wasn't especially clear. The Germans considered several policies. In July 1940 they decided to send all German and West European Jews to the island of Madagascar, which is just off the east coast of Africa. However, once it became clear that the war with Britain would go on into 1941, this plan had to be abandoned.

Germany was still carrying out other policies. In those countries in *western* Europe which Germany now controlled, such as France, Jews could emigrate if they were citizens (or married to citizens) of neutral countries, such as the USA. This policy remained in place until October 1941. For the Jews of *eastern* Europe, though, treatment was already very different.

'SPECIAL ACTION'

Polish Jews were forced into **ghettos** in the eastern part of Poland. Conditions were so bad that between 1939 and 1941 perhaps as many as 600,000 out of Poland's 2 million Jews died in these ghettos and camps. It seems, though, that even as late as June 1941, the Nazi leaders were still not sure just what solution they had in mind for the 'Jewish Question'. The German invasion of Russia in that month forced them to make up their minds.

Special Action Squads (*Einsatzgruppen*) were set up. To begin with, these squads didn't usually kill Jewish women and children. One squad's detailed records show that in July 1941 they executed 4,293 Jews. Only 135 of these were women. In September, though, the same squad killed 56,459 Jews. Among these were over 41,000 women and children.

At some point during the autumn of 1941, Hitler decided that all of Russia's 5 million Jews, and any others in German hands, would have to die. Hitler told Himmler, head of the SS, to find a way of doing it. Clearly, execution by rifle fire was too slow and messy. It would not be long before Himmler came up with a solution.

Q

1. Explain how and why Nazi policy towards the Jews changed between 1939 and October 1941.

2. The Nazis tried to carry out massacres like the ones described in these sources in secret. Why do you think they tried to keep the evidence of these crimes hidden?

3. The German, Hermann Graebe, who witnessed the killings in **Source A** was a civilian engineer, not a soldier. He noted the event in his diary but made no protest. Do you think he shares some of the blame for events like the one he witnessed?

Check out the link:
Look at Chapter 6. How were the problems in the ghettos caused by the Nazi treatment of the Jews in the years 1939–41?

6 WHAT WAS LIFE LIKE IN THE GHETTOS?

CHECK OUT THE LINK
How did the Nazis treat the Jews in the early stages of the war? (Chapter 5)

THE SETTING UP OF THE GHETTOS

Germany's successful invasion of Poland in September 1939 hugely increased Germany's territory and the number of people under its control. Eighteen million Poles and 2 million Jews now fell under German rule. Part of this territory would make up what was now called Greater Germany. A further part – called General Government – was set aside as a 'dumping ground' for Poles, Jews and Gypsies. As the Poles and Jews were forced from their homes in Greater Germany, Germans were moved in.

Once they were in the General Government, the Jews were made to live in small sections of cities or towns, called ghettos. The Germans then sealed off these ghettos with a three-metre-high wall so that nobody could get in or out without permission. The commanders of these ghettos were not sure what would happen to the Jews. Some Nazis wanted them to be left to starve to death, others argued that they could be made to work for the German economy by making goods, such as shoes and furniture.

NEW WORDS

DEPORTATION: the forced removal of a group of people from one place to another.
DYSENTERY: an infection of the intestines leading to severe diarrhoea. Death is caused by dehydration (loss of fluids).

SOURCE A

▲ Map of Greater Germany, 1941.

LIVING CONDITIONS IN THE GHETTO

In October 1940 the Germans ordered all of Warsaw's 400,000 Jews to live in the Jewish district of Warsaw. The ghetto made up less than 3 per cent of the city's area but a third of the city's population now had to live there. The accommodation became vastly overcrowded, with six or seven people to a room. By March 1941, a further 100,000 Jews had been brought in, raising the population of the ghetto to 500,000.

Only 1 per cent of the apartments in the Warsaw ghetto had running water, and fuel and food were in very short supply. Smuggling food into the ghetto – or leaving it without permission – meant immediate execution. The Jews were allowed a food ration of 300 calories a day; Poles outside the ghetto got 600 and Germans 2,300.

The minimum to keep a person alive is 2,000 a day. Warsaw's Jews survived only because of the smuggling in of food from outside the ghetto.

OPERATION REINHARD

From July 1942, however, the problem of overcrowding began to get less severe. From then on the Jewish council had to provide the names of 10,000 people each day for what was called 'resettlement'. The Germans told the Jews that they were being 'resettled' in work camps further east. In fact, they were being sent to the new death camps which the Nazis had just begun to build. This mass gassing of Jews in the General Government was called 'Operation Reinhard'. At first many went willingly, desperate to escape the ghetto – in 1941 more than 1,000 Jews a week were dying from diseases such as dysentery and typhus (see page 2) as well as hunger. But as rumours began to spread about what was happening to these Jewish families, volunteers became more and more scarce.

SOURCE B

▲ *Jews in the ghetto.*

SOURCE C

A few babies were born in the ghetto but, for one reason or another, their lives were very brief as this extract makes clear. Both the doctor and nurse were Jews.

And when the baby was born, the doctor handed it to the nurse, and the nurse laid it on one pillow, and smothered [suffocated] it with another [pillow]. The baby whimpered for a while and then grew silent. This woman was nineteen years old. The doctor didn't say a thing to her. Not a word. And this woman knew herself what she was supposed to do.

▲ *Quoted in* **Courage under Fire: Disease, Starvation and the Death in the Warsaw Ghetto,** *by C.G. Roland (1992).*

Q **1.** Using the sources and the text, describe the conditions in the ghettos. Mention:
- Overcrowding
- Disease
- Starvation
- Fear of **deportation**

2. Using **Source A**, explain why the Nazis chose cities like Warsaw and Lodz as ghetto areas for deported Jews.

3. Do you think the nurse who suffocated the baby in **Source C** was guilty of murder? Give reasons for your answer.

4. Some historians claim that the Nazis planned from the beginning of the war to murder all of Europe's Jews. What evidence can you find in Chapters 5 and 6 which disagrees with this view?

Check out the link:

Look at Chapter 7. How did conditions in the ghettos help lead to the Final Solution?

7 WHAT WAS THE FINAL SOLUTION?

CHECK OUT THE LINK
What was life like in the camps? (Chapter 9)

THE WANNSEE CONFERENCE

In January 1942, a group of leading Nazis met at Wannsee, just outside Berlin. Here Reinhard Heydrich, the man in charge of the Special Action Squads, discussed how Europe's Jews would be murdered. Adolf Eichmann (the head of the Gestapo dealing with Jewish affairs) drew up a list showing where, according to his statistics, all of Europe's 11 million Jews lived, including 330,000 in Britain. The Wannsee Conference, which lasted only 90 minutes, did not start the Holocaust. That was already taking place. But it did represent the point when it became official government policy. From now on, the mass murder of all of Europe's Jews would be planned in great detail.

The Conference decided that some Jews – the fit and strong – would be spared for a few months to work for Germany. All those who were of no immediate use – the old, the very young and their mothers, the sick – would be sent for 'special treatment'. The official report of the conference did not directly use the words 'murder' or 'gassing'. It talked about 'resettling'. The Conference didn't make a decision over the fate of mixed-race Jews. These were Jews with two or more Aryan grandparents. As a result, the vast majority of these half-Jews survived the war.

GAS VANS

Himmler was determined to carry out the order of the **Führer** as efficiently as possible. He had witnessed a mass-shooting in Russia which did not impress him. It was messy – Himmler got spattered with the brains of one victim who had been shot in the head – and it was slow. The Nazis had already experimented 'successfully' with gas vans. Nearly 100,000 victims had been gassed to death in sealed vans, using carbon monoxide exhaust fumes from the engine. But these vans could only take about 30 victims at a time and the vans had to drive around for about 30 minutes to be sure that everyone had been suffocated.

An eye witness account of a gassing by an SS officer, ➤ Kurt Gerstein, of a gassing in August 1942, at Belzec. Gerstein was horrified by what he saw. He wrote this account in 1945 before he killed himself.

NEW WORDS

CREMATORIUM: a place where bodies are burned.
EXTERMINATION: total destruction; in this case of Europe's Jews.
FÜHRER: all-powerful leader; this was the title given to Hitler since 1934.

SOURCE A

At last, after thirty-two minutes, they are all dead … The dead stand like pillars pressed together in the chambers. There is no room to fall or even to lean over. Even in death one can tell which are the families. They are holding hands in death and it is difficult to tear them apart in order to empty the chambers for the next batch. The corpses are thrown out with sweat and urine, smeared with excrement and menstrual blood on their legs. The corpses of children fly through the air. There is no time … Two dozen dentists open the mouths and look for gold … Some of the workers check genitals and anus for gold, diamonds and valuables.

SOURCE B

◄ *Map of the main concentration and extermination camps.*

DEATH FACTORIES

In early 1942 the SS set up the first death camps in the General Government area of Poland. Among these camps were Belzec, Sobibor and Treblinka. These camps were used only for mass murder. It was to these camps that the Jews from the ghettos in Poland were taken. Other camps, like Auschwitz, had both labour and **extermination** sections. The Jews arrived by train in trucks normally used for cattle. The SS target was to gas the transported Jews within two hours. For things to go as smoothly as possible it was vital that there were no scenes of panic or chaos. The victims had to be unaware of what was going to happen to them.

The SS, therefore, made a great effort to calm their victims. The SS wanted the Jews to believe that Treblinka had a real railway station and that they would stay in the camp for a few days before being sent further east for 'resettlement', where they would be put to work. There were signs for a 'ticket office' and 'restaurant'. The truth was that Treblinka was the end of the line.

THE MATHEMATICS OF MURDER

Treblinka could 'process' (another SS term for murder) 1,000 prisoners an hour. The SS worked a 12-hour shift. Auschwitz was the first camp to use Zyklon B. This gas came in cyanide crystal form. The crystals were sprinkled into the gas chamber through openings in the roof. The five chambers at Auschwitz could 'process' 2,000 people at a time. The heat from the bodies packed into the chamber helped the crystals give off a poisonous vapour which caused death by suffocation within ten minutes. The chamber was then ventilated so that a squad of prisoners could enter. The bodies were then taken to the **crematoria** where they were burned.

SOURCE C

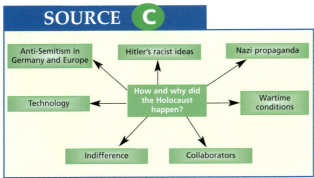

▲ *Spidergram: How the Final Solution happened.*

Q

1. Look at the map in **Source B**. What reason can you suggest for why almost all the killing centres were built in what used to be Poland? (clue: think about where most of the victims came from).

2. The man who wrote **Source A** was an SS officer – the very people who carried out these murders. Do you think we should believe what he has to say? Explain your answer.

3. Using the evidence of sources and the text in this chapter (and any others which may help), describe the stages which led to the Final Solution. The spidergram in **Source C** will help you put your information in order.

8 WHO WERE THE OTHER VICTIMS OF THE HOLOCAUST?

CHECK OUT THE LINK
Why did Hitler hate the Jews? (Chapter 5)
What was life like in the camps? (Chapter 9)

NEW WORDS

SLAVS: the Slavic group of peoples, which includes Russians, Poles, Czechs, Bulgarians and Serbs.

THE NAZI HATE LIST

The list of groups hated by the Nazis is a long one. Jews were at the top of the list but there were many others. About 18 million Europeans became prisoners of Hitler's Germany. At least 11 million of these died and 6 million of them were Jews. Who were these other 5 million men, women and children?

The Nazis graded their victims, according to how much they hated them. Each of the groups was forced to wear a symbol on their prison uniforms (see **Source A**). Jews were top of the list. For them, there was no hope. Death, sooner rather than later, was certain. For the others, there could be death by gassing or starvation, disease or overwork. But many would also survive. They would all be badly treated but death was not certain.

After the Jews came the Gypsies. When the gas chambers were no longer full of Jews, the Nazis would find space for many of them as well. Homosexuals were also persecuted. The Nazis despised homosexuals, even if they were pure Germans. Homosexuals refused to have children and therefore they couldn't carry out their duty to continue the race.

THE FATE OF SLAV CHILDREN

The list went on and on. Priests, nuns, Jehovah's Witnesses, Communists – anyone whose Christian faith or political beliefs led them to reject Nazism – all were also sent to the camps. The Germans thought **Slavs** were inferior but they had a use for them. They would be used as slave labour to help Germany win the war. If millions of them died in the process, well, that wouldn't matter. About three million Russian prisoners of war died in German hands. The Germans carried out medical experiments on some, like the one in **Source C**.

Some of the very young Slav children would be spared. If they looked Aryan and had the necessary blue eyes and blonde hair they would be taken from their parents and sent to Germany. Here German couples who had no children would adopt them. The Nazis kidnapped 200,000 Polish children but not all were as lucky as these. Some girls between the ages of 8 and 12 were given hormone injections

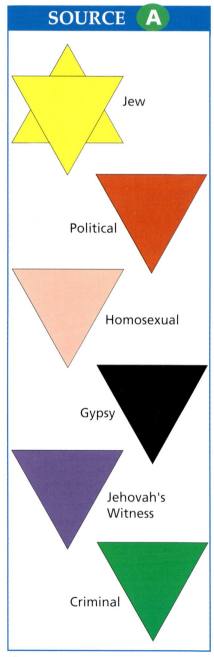

SOURCE A

Jew

Political

Homosexual

Gypsy

Jehovah's Witness

Criminal

▲ *The symbols worn by camp prisoners.*

so that they reached puberty more quickly. Then they were made pregnant. After they had had three or four children, they were killed.

GYPSIES

Gypsies became a target for Nazi hatred for one major reason. The Nazis disapproved of the way they lived. They didn't live at one fixed address or have regular jobs. This meant, the Nazis argued, that they couldn't contribute to the process of making Germany a great nation again. Therefore, what decided whether someone was a Gypsy was their heritage and the way they lived.

In December 1942 Himmler ordered all Gypsies to be sent to Auschwitz. To begin with, they were treated better than the Jews. They weren't gassed and families were allowed to stay together and made to work. Despite this, perhaps a quarter of the Gypsy population under German control perished in the Nazi camps. This would have been about 220,000 men, women and children. In the end, some were gassed, others were shot and many died of disease and hunger.

SOURCE B

Not only the Jews but also the gypsies were the victims of experiments. Vera Alexander recalled how two gypsy twins, one a hunchback, had been sewn together and their veins connected by Mengele who concentrated on blood transfusions in many experiments. 'Their wounds were infected,' she said, 'and they were screaming in pain. Their parents managed to get hold of some morphine [pain-killing drug] and used it to kill them in order to end their suffering.'

▲ One of the many experiments carried out by Dr Mengele – the doctor with the worst record for cruel medical experiments in the camps.

SOURCE C

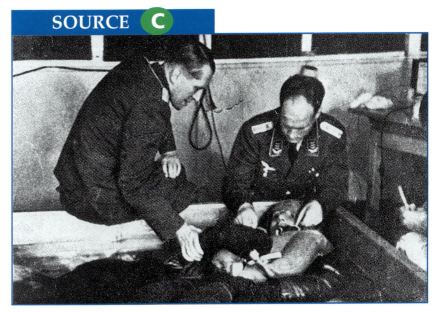

▲ A prisoner, wearing the clothes of a German pilot, is kept in a tank of freezing water to see how long he can survive. These 'doctors' were also keen to discover what was the best way to revive someone rescued from freezing water. One method included pumping very hot water into their intestines, bladder and stomach. The victims always died.

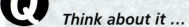

Q **Think about it …**
You have been asked by Heinrich Himmler, the head of the SS, to set out Nazi policy towards all those groups seen as enemies. In your report:

■ Identify who these groups are.

■ Explain why the Nazis see them as enemies of the new Germany.

■ Suggest how they should be treated.

Check out the link:
Look at Chapter 3. How did Hitler's ideas mean that Jews were not the only people persecuted by the Nazis?

9 WHAT WAS LIFE LIKE IN THE CAMPS? (Part 1)

CHECK OUT THE LINK
Who were the other victims of the Holocaust?
(Chapter 8)

NEW WORDS

TRANSPORT: a Nazi term used to describe a group of arrivals, usually by train, at a camp.

THE SELECTION

Some camps, like Auschwitz, had two roles. They were killing centres and they were work camps. When the cattle trucks arrived at the camp, the SS made a 'selection'. The SS commander checked the new arrivals as they filed past him. Those who looked over 15 and appeared strong and healthy were sent to the left. The old, the sick, pregnant women and women with young children were all sent to the right. On average about 10 per cent of a **transport** would be sent to the left. These were called 'work-Jews'. The rest made their way directly to their deaths in the gas chambers.

Those who had passed the selection could expect to live for about three months. This was how long the SS calculated people could survive on the rations they gave them. Every time a new transport arrived, the SS made another selection of work-Jews. Those who looked sick and weak were killed to make way for a new batch of work-Jews. Diseases like typhus also killed large numbers.

FOOD

In theory the daily food ration for a prisoner in a work camp was made up of 350 grams of bread, and half a litre of substitute coffee for breakfast. Lunch and supper was a litre of potato and turnip soup. Four times a week the soup was supposed to contain 20 grams of meat. In practice, workers never got anything like this. On average they got about 1,500 calories of food a day. The minimum calorie intake for survival for someone who isn't doing hard, physical work is 2,000 calories. From this it's easy to see why three months was about as long as a prisoner could expect to live.

You had to be cunning if you wanted to live for longer. It wasn't a good idea to be at the front of the queue for soup. Those at the front got the soup from the top of the cauldron. This was always thin and watery. The closer to the bottom your helping was, the better the chance it might contain some potato or turnip. Prisoners in work groups sometimes had the chance to smuggle in food from outside, but the punishment was severe as **Source D** shows. Neither was it sensible to be too fussy about what you ate, as **Source B** makes clear.

SOURCE A

Here is a woman – she walks quickly, but tries to appear calm. A small child with a pink cherub's face runs after her, and, unable to keep up, stretches out his little arms and cries: 'Mama! Mama!'.

'Pick up your child, woman!'

'It's not mine, sir, not mine!' she shouts hysterically, covering her face with her hands. She wants to hide, she wants to reach those who will not ride the trucks, those who will walk on foot, those who will stay alive … She wants to live.

▲ One prisoner described how one woman behaved when she realised that women with young children would be gassed. Quoted in This Way for the Gas, Ladies and Gentlemen, *by T. Borowski.*

SOURCE B

I will never forget a woman, I believe her name was Kleinova, who always used to carry her bread ration around with her, so that she would not die of hunger. One day her bread ration fell into the dirty toilet and out of sheer despair she crept into the pit, or it seems that she had let herself fall into it, to get her bread ration. Though she, and the bread, were disgustingly filthy, this was of no importance to her. The animal instinct to survive, by keeping food at hand, had won.

◄ *Judith was a 13-year-old Jewish girl when she was transported with her parents to Birkenau camp. This is taken from* Memories of My Childhood *by Judith Jaegerman (1985).*

SOURCE D

This is one of the drawings made by Zofja ➤ Rozenstrauch, a Polish prisoner in Auschwitz from 1943–45. They were used as evidence in the trial of one of the Nazi leaders, Adolf Eichmann, in 1961.

SOURCE C

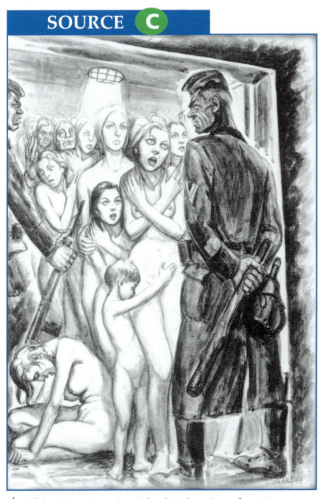

▲ *This drawing is titled* Selection for Gas Chambers, *by David Olere, a prisoner who was saved because his artistic talents were useful to the SS.*

Q Think about it …

1. Why were the SS confident that prisoners in a work camp like Birkenau would live for about three months?

2. Why would someone like David Olere be especially useful to a historian studying the Holocaust?

3. Look at each of the sources in this chapter. Which one do you think most sums up the horror of being a victim of the Holocaust? Give reasons for your choice.

WHAT WAS LIFE LIKE IN THE CAMPS? (Part 2)

DYING CONDITIONS

There were separate barracks for men and women but they were much the same. There were also separate sections for the different types of prisoner. Jews had the worst conditions and the worst food. Political prisoners, such as Communists, were normally better off. All prisoners wore a prison uniform which was made of cheap, flimsy material and soon became a dirty, smelly rag. In some camps, each prisoner had a bowl and a pair of wooden clogs.

Each morning the prisoners had to stand outside the barracks in their uniforms for hours at a time while the SS guards did a roll-call to see who had died during the night and to make sure there had been no escapes. Roll-calls, particularly in the freezing weather, often led to the deaths of the sick. Punishments were always done in public to set an example to the prisoners (see **Source E**).

The sleeping accommodation was in levels of bunks. The bunks were nothing more than planks of wood with gaps between them. There were no mattresses. The best level to sleep on was the top. Those on the lower levels had to deal with the problem of urine and diarrhoea dripping on them from the bunk above.

THE 'SCHINDLER JEWS'

Those Jews who were fit enough to work did a number of jobs. Some worked in quarries, breaking up rocks for use in building work. Others worked building roads or in factories making armaments or uniforms. The 1,200 Jews who worked for Oskar Schindler were supposed to be making weapons. None of the shells his factory made worked. But that was what Schindler wanted.

Oskar Schindler was a German and a member of the Nazi Party. He quickly saw that he could make a fortune from the war using cheap Jewish labour, and he did make

SOURCE E

The three victims mounted together onto the chairs. The three necks were placed at the same moment within the nooses. 'Long live liberty!' cried the two adults. But the child was silent.

'Where is God? Where is He?' someone behind me asked.

At a sign from the head of the camp, the three chairs tipped over …

Then the march past began. The two adults were no longer alive. Their tongues hung swollen, blue-tinged. But the third rope was still moving; being so light, the child was still alive ….

For more than half an hour he stayed there, struggling between life and death, dying in slow agony under our eyes. And we had to look him full in the face. He was still alive when I passed in front of him. His tongue was still red, his eyes were not yet glazed. Behind me, I heard the same man asking:

'Where is God now?'

And I heard a voice within me answer him:

'Where is He? Here He is – He is hanging here on this gallows …'

That night the soup tasted of corpses.

▲ *From* Night, *by Elie Wiesel (1982). The 15-year-old Wiesel was imprisoned in Auschwitz with his father.*

a fortune. But at some point during the war, he decided that he would use this fortune to save the lives of the Jews who worked in his factory. He was on very good terms with the SS and bribed them to leave 'his' Jews alone.

When the war ended, all 1,200 of them had survived, but Schindler had to escape from Europe because of his links with the SS and his membership of the Nazi Party. He tried to live in the USA but the government wouldn't let him in because he had been a member of the Nazi Party. He died in 1974 in Germany, remembered only by the people he had saved.

'THERE IS NO WHY'

Primo Levi was an Italian Jew who survived the Holocaust because he had a degree in chemistry and this was useful to the Germans, who were trying to make artificial rubber. In his book, *Survival in Auschwitz*, he probably came as close as anyone to explaining the reason for all the suffering (see **Source F**).

SOURCE G

It was common practice to remove the skin from dead prisoners. It was chemically treated and placed in the sun to dry. After that it was put into various sizes for use as saddles, riding breeches, gloves, house slippers and ladies' handbags. Tattooed skin was especially valued by SS men … Also we frequently got requests for the skulls or skeletons of prisoners. In this case we boiled the skull or the body … The SS men would say 'We will try to get you some with good teeth.'

▲ *An account by Dr Franz Blaha, one of seven doctors who carried out medical experiments at Dachau concentration camp.*

SOURCE F

Driven by thirst, I eyed a fine icicle outside the window, within hand's reach. I opened the window and broke off the icicle but at once a large, heavy guard prowling outside brutally snatched it away from me. 'Warum?' ('Why?') I asked him in my poor German. 'Hier ist kein warum,' ('Here there is no why'), he replied, pushing me inside with a shove.

▲ *Taken from* Survival in Auschwitz, *by Primo Levi (1993).*

SOURCE H

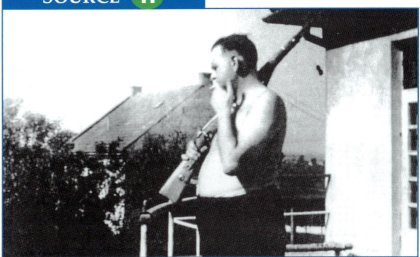

▲ *Amon Goeth, the commandant of Plaszow camp where Schindler's Jews spent some time. Goeth liked to spend his leisure time shooting 'slow' workers from his balcony.*

 Think about it …

1. Do you think the American government was right not to let Schindler live in the USA? Give reasons for and against their decision.

2. Judging from the evidence of **Source E**, some Jews stopped believing in God. Why do you think they did this?

3. 'Here there is no why.' What do you think the German guard in **Source F** meant when he said this? Consider the following points:

- How people were treated.
- How this would break all ideas of moral behaviour.
- What attitudes the Nazis had towards what was right and wrong.

10 WHY WAS THERE SO LITTLE OPPOSITION TO THE HOLOCAUST?

CHECK OUT THE LINK
What was life like in the camps? (Chapter 9)

RESISTANCE BY JEWS

A difficult question to answer is why didn't the Jews fight back? Why did so many millions go to their deaths with so little protest? To begin with, the Jews didn't know what was happening to them. They believed the Germans' lie that they were being sent from their ghettos to work in the east. Once they really understood what was happening, some did try to resist.

By January 1943 the Warsaw ghetto's Jewish population had fallen from 500,000 to just 60,000. The rest had been transported to the Treblinka death camp. The Jews formed a resistance group of one thousand men and women, each armed with a revolver. They had only ten rifles between them. After a month of bitter fighting in April 1943 the Germans crushed the revolt. About 14,000 Jews and 350 Germans were killed.

RESISTANCE IN THE CAMPS

The example of the rising by Jews in Warsaw inspired acts of revolt by Jews in the camps. Seven hundred Jews rebelled at the Treblinka camp and killed 15 SS guards but only 12 of the rebels escaped. In October 1943 a mass escape by 600 prisoners from Sobibor took place after ten guards had been killed. Once again, though, only 60 survived as most of those who escaped were handed over to the Germans by the local population. In October 1944, Jews blew up one of the gas chambers at Auschwitz. Some 250 escaped but they were all recaptured and shot.

NAZI REPRISALS

It isn't difficult to understand why there was so little help for Jews from non-Jewish civilians. Probably the most important reason is that many of the population of

SOURCE A

Jewish people, the hour is drawing near. You must be prepared to resist, not give yourselves up to slaughter like sheep. Not a single Jew should go to the railroad cars. Those who are unable to fight must go into hiding … Our slogan must be: All are ready to die like human beings.

▲ *A statement by ZOB (a Jewish resistance group) in January 1943, found in* The Jews of Warsaw, 1939–1943, *by Y. Gutman.*

Nazi-controlled countries shared the Nazi's hatred of the Jews. Some of them actually helped the SS to carry out the Final Solution and joined the Germans as policemen.

Others didn't share this hatred but were too frightened to help the Jews. The standard Nazi reprisal for any person hiding or feeding Jews wanted by the SS was death – death for the individual and his or her family. The vast majority, especially in places like Germany and those countries in western Europe controlled by the Germans, didn't hate the Jews to the extent that they would help murder them. On the other hand, there were those who actively collaborated and gave them away.

SOURCE B

▲ *Some Jews who did escape ended up in Jewish partisan groups, like this one.*

SOURCE C

▲ *Captured Jewish fighters after the Warsaw ghetto rising. Women, as you can see, were involved in the fighting as well. Some of the fighters were shot straightaway, others were sent to Treblinka.*

WHY DIDN'T THE ALLIES DO SOMETHING?

Why didn't Britain and the USA (the Allies) do something to stop the Holocaust? After all, they were at war with Germany and they did know what was happening. In June 1942 a British newspaper reported that the Germans had already murdered 700,000 Jews.

It must be said that the leaders of Britain and the USA did not see saving the lives of Jews in Europe as a priority. The main task was to defeat Germany. Only the defeat of Germany, they argued, would really save the Jews. The longer the war went on, the longer the Nazis could go on killing them. Besides, what could they have done? Auschwitz was too far away to bomb until 1944, and how many prisoners would have been killed in bombing raids?

Think about it …

Your task is to write an essay in answer to the question 'Why didn't the Jews fight back against the Nazis?' The essay is made up of five paragraphs. Each paragraph starts with an opening phrase. Your task is to complete the phrase and then provide any evidence you can find from this chapter.

Paragraph 1:

'One reason was because the Jews didn't know what was going to happen to them.

Paragraph 2:

'Once they were in the camps, there was little chance of escape. '(Use the evidence from the revolts at Treblinka, Sobibor and Auschwitz.)

Paragraph 3:

'There was also little chance of getting any help from the local population in Poland because …' (You could mention two reasons here.)

Paragraph 4:

'Besides, sometimes they did fight back. In April 1943 the Jews of the Warsaw Ghetto …' (Use **Source A** as well.)

Conclusion:

'The greatest reason why it was difficult for the Jews to resist was probably because…'

11 WHAT HAPPENED WHEN PEOPLE FOUND OUT ABOUT THE HOLOCAUST?

THE DESTRUCTION OF EVIDENCE

In 1944 the Germans became worried by the advance of the Russian army into eastern Europe. In September of that year they decided to start moving their prisoners from the camps in Poland to camps in the west. As many as 100,000 prisoners died on the journey by foot or railway. In November, Himmler ordered that all gassings should stop and that the gas chambers be destroyed. There was to be no evidence of the extermination methods.

Prisoners continued to die by the tens of thousands but from disease, overwork and starvation. The last roll-call in Auschwitz was on January 17, 1945. There were precisely 67,012 prisoners. The Germans decided to move to Germany almost all of these to avoid the advancing Russians. The ones they left behind were too sick to bother with. When the Russians entered the camp on January 27, they found 2,800 half-dead victims.

British troops also came across the camps. In April 1945 they entered Belsen. With them was a BBC reporter, Richard Dimbleby. His filmed broadcast (see **Source A**) about what he saw stunned the British people as they began to realise what crimes their enemy had committed.

THE NUREMBERG TRIALS

The British, American and Soviet governments decided that the men and women who ran these camps and organised the Final Solution were guilty of war crimes and crimes against humanity. The trials took place at Nuremberg in Germany. Some, like Himmler, Goebbels, Goering and, of course, Hitler, killed themselves before they could be executed. Ten other leading Nazis were hanged in 1946. Among the last words spoken by one of these, Julius Streicher, were 'Heil Hitler'.

Not all those involved in these war crimes got as far as a trial. In many cases, camp commanders and guards were simply executed by enraged Allied soldiers. Some of these guards tried to escape by dressing up in prisoners' uniforms but their well-fed, healthy appearances gave them away.

THE HOLOCAUST TODAY

The amount of historical evidence that the Holocaust took place as described in this book is massive: the eye witness accounts, the photographs, the remains of the camps. Yet there are a few people today who claim that the Holocaust

SOURCE B

The claim that the Holocaust never happened has been spreading in America. The statement becomes more respectable as it is passed along, especially to the young. A Jewish mother from the mid-west of America hired a 15-year-old non-Jewish girl to help with the children one summer. The mother had a number of books on her shelves about the Holocaust. The bright 15-year-old said one day, in a nice way, as if she was stating a simple fact: 'Why do you have so many books on that? It never happened, you know.'

▲ *From an article by Lance Morrow in* Time *magazine, entitled 'Never Forget', April 26 1993.*

Q *Think about it …* Some people, who are not racist or anti-Semitic, argue that it is time to forget about the Holocaust because it happened a long time ago, and it isn't relevant to the world today. Instead, we should think about the many terrible events which are happening now. Do you agree or disagree with this view?

was invented by the Allies after the war and never happened. These people are called 'Holocaust deniers'. Some, like David Irving, claim that although some Jews were killed during the war, they weren't gassed because there were no gas chambers. The chambers in the camps, he claims, were not for gassing the Jews to death but for killing the lice on them after the Jews' arrival at the camp.

In April 2000 a British court decided that Irving had twisted historical evidence to suit his 'pro-Nazi' and 'anti-Semitic and racist' views. This decision will not put a stop to the claims of these new Nazis. These people will continue to believe what they want to believe, and they will continue to ignore the evidence of history.

SOURCE C

▲ *Victims of Buchenwald concentration camp.*

12 HOW AND WHY DID THE HOLOCAUST HAPPEN?

The history web on page 7 told you what the key questions were which we needed to answer to explain how and why the Holocaust happened. We have now investigated each of these questions. The time has come to put these individual investigations together to arrive at an overall answer to the question at the top of this page.

We can identify seven broad reasons which explain how and why the Holocaust happened. These are set out in **Source A**.

SOURCE A

How and why did the Holocaust happen?		
Basic reason	Explanation	Evidence to support this reason
Many people were indifferent to the Jews	This means many people just stood by without doing anything to help the Jews because they didn't care about them.	(Look in Chapter 10)
Nazi propaganda	Once the Nazis were in power, they began to turn the German people against the Jews and passed many laws against them.	(Look in Chapters 3 and 4)
Wartime conditions	However, the Nazis couldn't really harm the Jews while there was peace in Europe. Once the war started, the Nazis could step up their campaign against the Jews.	One of the first things they did was start moving Jews into special ghettos in Poland. (Look in Chapters 5, 6 and 10)
Collaborators	The Nazis found it easier to carry out their policies because they were helped by other people who shared their hatred of the Jews. These people are called collaborators.	(Look in Chapter 10)
Hitler's racist ideas	Hitler made the most of this anti-Semitism. He added to it by making more claims against the Jews.	(Look in Chapters 1 and 3)
Technology	The Nazis would always have found ways to murder some Jews but the use of modern technology such as gas made it possible for them to kill millions, not just thousands.	(Look in Chapter 7)
Anti-Semitism in Germany and Europe	There had always been people in Germany and Europe who hated the Jews.	Some people blamed the Jews for the death of Christ. (Look in Chapter 3)
Conclusion	The Holocaust could never have happened without the war.	

▲ *How and why did the Holocaust happen: outline of reasons.*

SOURCE B

▲ *How and why did the Holocaust happen: essay structure chart.*

SOURCE C

▲ *Justice: the execution of a Nazi war criminal, Alfred Klein, by the Americans. He ordered the murder by injection of 475 Polish and Russian civilians.*

Q Think about it …

1. Your task is to write a short essay in answer to the question: 'How and why did the Holocaust happen?' To begin with, it's a good idea to put these reasons together into two groups. The first group is the reasons which existed before the war, and the second group is the reasons which came about only because of the war.

Look at **Source A**.

■ Write down the reasons which you think already existed before the war.

■ Write down all the other reasons which came about because of the war.

Are there any which might belong to both groups?

2. Now you need to start gathering the evidence to support these points. **Source B** provides a chart which you can copy out and fill in with the evidence for each of the points you have written down for Q1. A couple of examples have already been done for you.

3. It's time, now, to put it all together into an essay. You have eight paragraphs to write. These are the seven reasons in **Source B**, plus the conclusion. This is your last paragraph to conclude or finish your essay. You could finish by explaining why the Holocaust couldn't have happened without there being a war (see **Source B**). It's always a good idea to try to make your paragraphs link together. For example, you can see from **Source B** that the paragraph about Hitler's racist ideas clearly follows on from the one about anti-Semitism in Germany and Europe.

Start your essay with the following introduction:

'The Holocaust happened for many reasons. Some of these were long-term reasons that had existed for many years – even centuries. These combined with short-term reasons which came about as a result of the Second World War.'

Now go on to develop the detailed points in these long- and short-term groups, finishing with a conclusion which shows that the war was the final trigger which allowed the Holocaust to happen.

INDEX